M000317614

how do you spell the sound of crickets

how do you spell the sound of crickets

poems in conversation

Paola Bruni & Jory Post

No part of this book may be reproduced or transmitted in any form or by any means, electronic or mechanical, except for the purpose of review and/or reference, without explicit permission in writing from the publisher.

Grateful acknowledgement is made to Nicholas Coley for the use of his original oil painting, *Atmospheric River*, on the cover. nicholascoley.com

Cover design by Marcus Eisendorf

Paola Bruni photograph by Annie Rowland
Jory Post photograph by Karen Wallace

Published by Unruly Voices, unrulyvoices.com
an imprint of Paper Angel Press, paperangelpress.com
copyright © 2022 Paola Bruni and Jory Post.
All rights reserved.
Manufactured in the United States of America
Printed on acid-free paper

ISBN 978-1-957146-38-6 (Trade Paperback)
10 9 8 7 6 5 4 3 2 1
FIRST EDITION

Before it all gets wiped away, let me say,
there is wisdom in the slender hour
which arrives between two shadows.

Li-Young Lee

contents

preface

"Write to me. Keep me alive." These words—this injunction I received from my friend Jory Post at the end of his life, are the heart of the twenty-three poems that make up this volume.

Jory and I met in Clifford Henderson's writing salon in Santa Cruz in the mid-2000s. Every week for nearly a decade, we sat in our respective chairs scribbling away and listening to each other read our work. We didn't socialize much, but we enjoyed each other's writing.

Eventually, the two of us found ourselves in Danusha Laméris's poetry group. Jory had been diagnosed with inoperable pancreatic cancer, and I was swimming in the grief of having recently lost my parents to illness. Our friendship found a foothold, as we were, each in our own way, forced to confront death.

In the summer of 2019, we both attended the Catamaran Writing Conference. Our instructor, the poet Dorianne Laux, conducted a lesson on epistles—specifically letter writing in poetic form. At the conclusion of the lesson, Dorianne circled the room, pairing students as partners, and suggested we "give it a try" on our own. As soon as Jory and I were matched, he was quick to throw down the gauntlet: "Let's write fifty poems before I'm gone. Twenty-five each. We can do this."

And so, we began our correspondence in the fall of 2019, a little more than a year before Jory passed away. But it is not his end that I want to talk about here. I want to talk about what it was like to exchange words and thoughts with a man who existed in a kind of oneiric limbo, a place of transcendent insight and inner glory.

For that is how I experienced Jory during those final months. His writing, always evocative and intelligent prior to his illness, developed a diaphanous, atmospheric quality as he underwent treatment. Jory's words lifted me into a musical netherworld where his ideas and inspirations not only played out on the page but entered my dreams.

I'll admit there were times I felt burdened by the strange and complex weight of our writing. I struggled to find meaningful and honest words—words that satisfied a need I had to offer empathy, healing. I stomped around my house, exasperated. I didn't want to be sentimental or sad. I didn't want to be inhibited. Easier said than done.

If we are truly lucky in this life, we discover people who hold a vision of us as more courageous and talented than we believe ourselves to be. Jory was one of these people for me. He cajoled and provoked, commanded me via e-mail to "stop what you're doing and write." Even while reporting "my oncologist's most commonly used word today is *failure*."

I believe that Jory was placed upon this earth to write. And his diagnosis, albeit tragic, tore away any last vestiges of doubt he had about this purpose. Despite nausea, pain, and fatigue, he filled journals with notes about his experiences. On any given day, a note was transformed into a sonnet, an essay, or a short play.

Although these poems represent just a fraction of Jory's literary work, he wrote, "I think it will be the most important I will complete during this time." Perhaps because our writing was a shared effort. Perhaps because we spoke to each other about unspeakable things on the page.

I wish Jory were here to witness the fruition of this project, the epistles wrought between us, as they move into the world, and develop a life of their own.

Paola Bruni
January 2022

I.

it's about our names

How they tax the brains of friends, acquaintances, total strangers. How they don't melt off tongues as easily as butterscotch candies, find their way into our writing as idioms and clichés, how they want to fight back and tell folks to pay attention. That it's not Paula, or Paul, or Paolo. But "Paola!" Say it! Like this! "Pow-Lah!" Repeat it five times. Look into my eyes. Do you see the twinkle there? Do you see the spark of life that is me? The me that can only be connected to someone named "Paola!"

Or mine. As you say, it's so simple: Joe-Ree. But for some strange reason it's the "J" that throws people off. Maybe it's the loop at the bottom, a slide down the shaft, and a catapult off the little hook that shoots them out into neverland. Gets them floating in the world of alternative consonants that create a "Cory" and a "Rory" and a "Gory." Or Georgie.

For eighteen years I hated my name. Had to retell the story about my mom being 8.5 months pregnant as she and my dad watched a contestant sign in to the Groucho Marx show: J-O-R-Y, a Scandinavian who pronounced it Jori. The shy guy that I was in every classroom being pointed out as having a unique name, when I would rather take my appointed place under a rock with the snakes and lizards.

How about you, my dear friend Paola? Did you always love your name? Your Italian heritage? Did you enjoy standing out in a crowd? Or were there too many of them? Was it as common as Joe or Sam? Jane and Mary?

Then there's the now. Where our names, our spirits, our lives, are beacons, attract others, force us to stand up and smile at the camera. Put our arms around others and give a deep, genuine hug. Paola and Jory. The brightness. The reflections. That which is out of our control.

J.P.

first things first: my family

Family. A word carried in steerage across the Atlantic,
        fear, longing, expectation accumulating
            under the skin,
      the salt of immigration held fast to the chest.

The plan: a home, sans the complication of Nazi infiltration,
        incendiary explosions, the broken mouths of history
          laying corpses in the road.

In America, my sister is first-born and forgiven her sex.
I am to be the son, Paolo, destined to stay the family
      name from extinction.

But I was born a girl,
        christened "Paola," meaning small. Paola,
           a name that stumps
      the English-speaking, causes tongues to twist,
          small embolisms to form in the brain.

In America, I am de-latinized, stripped
        of my exotic reverberation.
      Paula. Payola. Polly. Pabla. Paoli.
         Mispronunciation, a persistent eddy.

Father's languor reflected in the sole use of my given name
to communicate disappointment, punishment, exile.

As a girl, I erred on the side of logic,
        rationalizing I could fashion myself into the boy
          he wanted.

Isn't that what all children do?
Give ourselves over to the gods of our birthing?
        Cloy and carve, amputate, reassemble?

I mixed concrete, pounded nails,
        wielded wrenches and screwdrivers, could slip
            a sharp wrist into an engine block.

Should I have questioned even my nickname, Pinky?
Recognized it as demoralizing? Less than? Not enough?

        But no. I held that name like redemption.
        It didn't carry the stigma of failure.
        Pinky is a name with a legacy.

Pinky Agnew, an actress from New Zealand. Pinky Tomlin,
    a singer. Pinky May, an American Major League Baseball player.
    Even Benazir Bhutto, the twice Prime Minister of Pakistan,
    was nicknamed Pinky.

My mother never called me Pinky. Not once.
        Said the name tasted wrong in her mouth like oil
        gone rancid. When breast cancer claimed
            her, I laid down my nickname.

But my family balked. I became Sister, Auntie,
    or She, Her.

Will they ever call me by my name?

P.B.

second things second:
a three-month gestation

I am guilty of producing way too much, and not nearly enough. If I grew, harvested, and squashed avocados into guacamole for all my friends, minced garlic, squeezed lemons, diced tomatoes and green onions, added the perfect amount of jalapeno, made homemade chips from scratch, used pink Himalayan salt, gorged everyone I know with my favorite appetizer, I'd still think of kids in the Central Valley and Watsonville who go hungry most nights.

I write. A lot. I mine phrases and idioms from fleshy pockets on my thighs, single words like saffron and arugula from my tongue where the tip taps the roof of my mouth, uncovers hidden flavors, tastes that morph into fragments, incomplete sentences, trilogies. I fill small journals, jumbo notebooks, scraps of napkins, hunt for light bulbs to illuminate my future, write scenes, conversations, descriptions, sometimes happily tell way more than I show.

I polish and edit and chop and add, deconstruct how and when Harry met Sally, reconstruct my incomplete world through research when I don't recognize Michelangelo's marbled rendition of Mary holding Jesus in her lap, turn paragraphs into chapters with titles that represent Greek gods or the children of the old lady in the shoe, find myself on page 320 of my electronic journal on the morning of November 5th, attempting to fill another gap, fulfill an obligation, soothe a desire.

I force myself into situations that modify my DNA, twist bones around muscle in unnatural unions, like the vocal class taught by the classically trained Shakespearean actor, like the writers' conference in Pebble Beach where Dorianne Laux asked us to understand the structure and voice of poetry through listening to rather than seeing words, where she paired us with classmates to form an epistolary partnership rooted in poetry, creating and sharing epistles.

I understand how first things come first. A match to kindling, followed by flame. Courtship that leads to cake and garters. A marriage building to separation, divorce, splinters under fingernails. I often avoid the first things first. Productive procrastination. Create so much that intentionally misses the point that it pretends to have been the point. I have yet to unveil what has been waiting for me since the beginning, hiding in plain sight.

By definition, second things tend to remain second. Like this poem for my epistolary partner, three months in utero. Festering under a flap of grey matter. Trying to fight its way to fingertips, make its way to paper, share itself through a small window that opens onto the universe. That it sprouts now, works its way to closure, becomes ready to share, alerts me once again to that unnamed first, hovering above, patiently waiting for its due focus.

J.P.

the needle

I've made friends with a needle.
>A sewing needle to be precise. Petite, with an elongated
>eye. One I can thread without squinting or steadying
>the slight tremor in my right hand.

The storm swirled on the Big Island. My sister and me, sequestered
>in a second story condo, red flag closures
>posted on all the beaches, black
>>skull warnings on some.
>Outside, record-breaking waves plunged
>>into the lava rock shore, rocketed skyward.

We slipped windows shut against the racket,
>turned to a pile of fabrics and threads,
>>a book on basic stitches.

I was intimidated at first. The needle, a tiny spear pricking
>my thumb and forefinger, reminding me of the finger
>>pricks you've endured, the infusions of poison
>meant to ward off disease and evil spirits.

You say you force yourself into situations
>to modify your DNA.
>I was doing it too by attempting to sew against my aversion.

As a girl, I wanted to love what the women
>in my family loved.
>But I was drawn outdoors
>>to the dirt. I wanted the world under my fingers
>>to push back, not yield.

I recall the heavy serrated shears, fabric shimmying
from my hands, failure to ride a level stitch.
Grandmother's admonishment.

At the condo, I pressed myself into intention.
Straight stitch first, then a backstitch. A chain
and a knot. Some things do come first.

I wanted to leap forward, avoid humiliating mishaps,
sew the swanky corset in the book, embellished
with maple leaves and curly stems.

I wanted to live somewhere other than the present.
And still, I was led back to the beginning.
Pierce the fabric, tug the needle.
Coax the thread. Repeat. Repeat. Repeat.

P.B.

go forth!

Go forth with epistolary panache
Melt your heated words on hungry fingers
Hunt and procure that which feeds blind desire
Prepare a feast to silence kings and queens
Filet of unicorn with mustard greens
Aardvark soup steamed over fresh volcano
Molten lava lizard cake on whipped clouds
Stand the known world on its head:
Ride a rhinoceros into the veldt
Capture fireflies on the tip of your tongue
Hide Easter eggs for unborn grandchildren
Shoot skyrockets from flaming eye sockets
Foretell futures through wrinkles in foreheads
Belly laugh loudly every chance you get.
Laugh loudly from the belly of the beast.

J.P.

shelter

I wonder whether a poem contains a ceiling, walls,
        an escarpment of words able to keep us safe.
            But there's no safety, is there?

In poems, you can bump up against things, like unicorn filet
        and aardvark soup, molten lava lizard cake,
            things that cause your mind to wander.

I need to wander right now. Escape the calisthenics of anxiety.

Although I am meant to be sheltered at home, I'm on the beach
        at sunrise like every other day. Seacliff State Beach,
            site of the concrete relic SS *Palo Alto*. Warship.
            Amusement park.
        Four-piece wreck, lying on her starboard side,
            stern torn clear off.

Normal is a trudge across damp sand. Sun bleeding golden guts
        into a cloudless sky. The ocean flipping
            icy foam onto the shore. Gulls that plunk
              into the waves, prowl trash bins.

I am guilty of taking in too much beauty.

People are dying, I tell myself.

A virus espaliers the globe, intent on infamy.
        But I've a copse of brain cells determined to wander

out to sea, jump into a sturdy skiff, find comfort
in discussing Chaucer with a tiger,
        or the effulgence of fairy tales.

Perhaps I'll string a waxy leg over a surfboard, coax a squealing
        catfish onto my lap, run my fingers over its pointy
                whiskers, quote the Upanishads.

I've never been good at being in a body.

The virus paints red and black crosses on doors,
        piles bodies in graveyards, buries mothers and fathers,
        grandparents. Buries friends and neighbors.

Reality is mathematical. Exponents and continents.
        Longitudes and latitudes. Statistics
                with their cold hard effigy.

Back at the house, Kip strums his Martin,
        croons *Woodstock* into a miniature mic,
        sets up virtual lessons for gaggles of high schoolers.

He's perched on the kitchen stool, a diffuse daylight glazing
        his skin an eerie bronze, salt and pepper hair shaggy.
                His voice is warm, glossy, insinuating
                        itself into my anatomy like an anchor.

P.B.

II.

what anchors release

Wrapped inside a fishing net, I ride the heavy iron to the sea floor, land in sand up to my knees, blow bubbles until they disappear. I wait, for an end of consciousness, for a catapult to the surface, for the teeth of a shark to rip the net or me, open, for something I've never seen or imagined. That's how I prefer to sink, waterlogged, a free fall accompanied by uncertainty. Not a darkness that paints me black, dyes me in the blue ink of squid, not one that demands I follow expected patterns and wrap myself tight in straightjackets and scream at walls. No, I seek. I know what I want. I visit shipyards, marinas, dry docks, harbors. Goldilocks on a hunt. A rusted hunk of metal that fits my body, allows me in, wraps itself around me. Together we find a pier, walk to the end. I lean, it pulls, we float, splash, plummet.

J.P.

between worlds

What is it about dreams?
Time without end. The dead feigning a Lazarus,
      returning in new, yet familiar skin.
      Levitation. Catastrophes survived.

In my dreams, I frequently
      drown in the blue, blue, nothing.
      Get swallowed whole.
      Then wake—a silvery thread, split-second
          realization—it was *just a dream.*

On Saturday, a raucous thunder yanked
      me from sleep around 2 a.m. It was a hot, angry
      bit of air howling like an injured brown buck. It sunk
      its teeth into my gut, had me pounding
          my ears with my fists. Sometimes, reality
             is too gritty, too gruesome.
      All that thunder wailing, echoing a kind of mortal pain.
          Is it your pain?
          Is it mine?

My neighbor works for the weather service, said the storm dropped
      right on us. No hesitation between illumination and grief.
          Like birth. First light, then loss.
      The sudden absence of a hospitable womb
      in exchange for the fierce interruption of life.

The storm took our sixty-foot redwood to task, stripped
      it down to a slender winter coat. My husband and I swept
          and swept, piling fronds.

I have no answers. And I'm weary of the effort
     to make sense of things.
       I'd rather dream, day and night.
         Live in dusky possibilities.

A few weeks ago, you appeared in my dream as a palimpsest,
     words and symbols trailing over your flesh, embossed
       watermarks rising, then fading away.

Outside the window, humpback whales surged.
     Porpoises frolicked under a glassy pink sun.
      I wanted to sleep forever, read the stories traveling
       across the flat shimmer of your eyes.

P.B.

more than two

So damn many worlds to discover and master. I find a new one every morning, riding a transparent wave in front of your collage-like dreams, fighting my way into a crack in the shell of a freshly hatched egg. Once inside, it's dark until I see the piercing light of your eyes illuminate our interior. This is one of those worlds. You hiding in the corner of this oval closet with your eyes wide open awaiting the next crack, the next catastrophe or miracle. You slip into a nearby stream of words inscribed on top of an ancient Tibetan etching, and I grab your ankle, join you, hands cupping water, this measured swim that empties us into a bay of your Capri as I roll onto my back and float to the shore of this place I've never been, a world whose mouths are full of romance and braggadocio. I sink into the moist sand, tiny crabs climbing over my chest treating me like Gulliver, cinching me down, tattooing me like a Rosetta stone to be interpreted by a future culture, restraining my desire to move on to what's pink and pure and unknown.

J.P.

returned

Capri? That first trip in '95 with Kip.
        A floating recognition, the stiff engine grate
                of the ferry boat on soft blue waves,
        l'isola rising like a misshapen pyramid
            in the distance.

The bay smelled of incense and hard history,
        the remains of disembodied Roman citizens
            rising up from the depths.

Once, Capri was under water,
        as I was once under water, fabrication
            of cells forming.
        How odd to think of life's early gestation,
            its innocent science and martial rule.

Did we have a choice about our bodies?
Would you have chosen yours?

Years in, and I'm still puzzled by the conflagration of flesh
        that binds my physiognomy—its bewildering
            sensitivities, near constant vertigo,
        random pains that sear my brain, send me weeping
            into the muffled dark.

Yet, unlike you, I have no known disease consuming
        me, no expiration foretold.

Can my memories of Capri shield you against
the spiraling indignities of the present?

Transport you from the wasteland of a body breaking?
My body thunders for Capri. My siren's heart harkening
through the liminal, as if all along
I've been waiting under water,
waiting for you to arrive.

You disembark from the ferry at Marina Grande,
postcard port of fishing boats and pleasure craft,
skiffs and half-rotting dinghies scraping
the old dock raw, a salty lament.

You hike the *Sentiero dei Fortini,* ruins of ancient
military outposts. Row the *Blue Grotto,* a cave
of azure phosphorescence. Ascend the 900-step
Scala Fenicia—climb to constellations.

At every Marian shrine, you make an offering: wildflowers, stones,
poems bent into ovals and hexagons—
the sacred geometry of your imagination.

Are you seeing what I see?
Can you feel the transparent waters?

P.B.

how do you spell
the sound of crickets?

Do they have crickets in Capri?
        I've never been.

It's your memories that drop me there.
        Place me on soil I've only dreamt about.

If crickets, do they speak the same language as ours?
        I imagine an Italian inflection, better at luring mates.

Not necessarily a softer entrance into the night.
        But a quicker exit.

I stay awake all night long listening to the stridulations of both.
        How do you spell the sound of crickets?

It's not so much that the answer is impossible to imagine.
        But rather that the question is impossible to pose.

I listen for syllables, try to slice out single letters.
        But the owl keeps asking who I am, what I want.

I seek this other worldly intrusion, a visitor to your island.
        I wince at my desire, know the crickets are the same
        everywhere.

I know the language of communication has been invented
by the human inhabitants.
        So we can better control the outcomes of our experience.

But we have no sway over those who speak with their wings.
    Our requests for invitations go ignored.

It's this thundering we all seek, not the claps filled with lightning bolts.
    Rather those stitched into the lining of our hearts.

We'll happily ride in on the shoulders of our friends
    Take this trek on uncharted soil.

Discover that the crickets of Capri are their own cousins.
    Will provide us with no solutions to unanswerable questions.

J.P.

this body yet lives

All the cricket wants is to eat and procreate.
      Symphonic chirp's steady grist—a mating call.
          With only months to live,
            life distilled into simple acts of genius.

I tried to make more of myself and failed.
Or my womb failed.
      Or my desire to be a mother failed.
          Or perhaps God knew I wouldn't survive
motherhood, the possibility of losing
        a whole person instead of an idea.

      Once, my guru said, *Miscarriage is a less conscious abortion.*
I recall the simple fear of carrying an embryo,
        strange sense of being inhabited,
           infernal power of making.

      I notch their ages in a molting of lost events,
            my first—37,
           the second, 18,
        with eyes and mouths,
      jumping legs, a set of wings for walking
and a pair for flying.

      This body still wants to eat and procreate.
Yet I can no longer make more of myself.
I rub my wings, chirp,
      sins and sorrows intact,
      make the sounds that say this body yet lives.

P.B.

III.

an imperfect draft

A draft appears again at the crack in the window in the middle of the night. It's not a perfect wind that blows in and wipes my mind, erases memories and futures I'd rather not see. It slides in crooked, random, with no intent. I want to think of it as a failure, that it lacks the strength to do what it is I'd like it to do. Would like to think of myself as a failure for allowing it in without my guidance. A breeze that blows piles of papers from their ordered stacks, rearranges my thoughts and words in ways I never would have imagined. A blast strong enough to knock paintings from walls, shatter glass into splinters on expectant carpets. Morphs into a soft breath that raises sheets, dances through the hair on my arms, raises questions. Inhabits me. Makes me its own, tosses me up and out of bed, throws me around the room, tries to squeeze me through the holes in screens. I scrape myself off the floor. Fight back. Recognize its imperfection. My own imperfections. Extend my months to live by laughing at us both. By crawling back under warm covers and staying horizontal until the next monsoon visits.

J.P.

how wind travels

You see how wind travels. How breath travels.
Amorphous yet visceral enough to pillage your papers,
       reorder your thoughts, send you careening
          into the walls of your room.

Is the wind empty? Full?
Or full only when it captures the burnished crepe of fall,
       wide-mouthed tongue of the sea,
       bedsheets pinched on clotheslines,
         'tis of thee flags with their
       undercurrent of propriety.

Perhaps when Neruda says, *con la mano recojo este vacio*
(with my hand, I gather in this emptiness),
       he speaks to the entangled particles
          that comprise atmosphere, aspiration, animas.

Emptiness—a secret the world keeps. I keep my secrets
       pastiched in a box, shelved in a book, buried
          in a subterranean cave, curtsying
              like a copse of English ladies at tea.
              Oh darling, did you hear about that poet?
              She's become obsessed with death.

You say you'll extend your months to live by laughing at us both.
Let us laugh, then.
       Keep the wind between us,
        two pearls churning the air, exhaling
a radiant surge of *Gloria in excelsis Deo.*

Let us listen to the wise man who writes:
What strikes the oyster shell does not damage the pearl.

P.B.

take me when I'm empty

Take me when I'm empty, can hide beneath a thumbprint or smudge on the mirror. Find me and rouse me when the small birds arrive, gentle in their flight, their landings, one seed at a time, a collaboration instead of a confrontation. When I'm flat and transparent is the time to lift me with thumb and index finger, make a home for me in a matchbox or the concave bed of a contact lens. Fill me with an eyedropper full of Orange Crush, caffeine, glucose, carbonation. Read to me from vials of words by Persian and Latin American poets. This is how you revive me, swim me to Capri, take me where you've been, carry me on your back, arm by arm I follow your movements, trust your instincts. The one-dimensional me wants to survive, wants to follow your memories to safe azure coves, wants you to help me expand, find my lost form. The me as poet hunts for more ways to stay alive than he does chasing or trying to understand death. What's to understand? A breath. One more breath. And another. One more line of Neruda or Rumi. Expand me, please. Keep me alive. One more poem added to the next.

J.P.

reduced to be remade

The finches slap themselves silly in the birdbath,
        pointed beaks shiny sharp.
                I want to hold their slick bodies,
        sense their bean-shaped lungs sucking air.
But the finches don't cooperate, nor do the sparrows
           or the other birds.

I worried about birds when the Santa Cruz Mountains
        flamed, atmosphere muddled to a burnt
           umber particulate.

At one point, when evacuation seemed possible,
        I said goodbye to things: antique dresser bought at auction
           decades ago, oval mirror with its fabled substrate,
                the custom-made desk
                    I'd waited a lifetime to deserve.

I ran my hands over the walls of my house with grief
        in my palms. Had I ever praised timber
and nails, sheetrock and insulation? Copper
        pipe and tangle of wires. Plaster and molding.
        Hinges and doorknobs.

You know, nothing of us burned.
        And though I'm tasting the air with less anxiety
        now, I still startle awake in the middle of the night
        expecting the elemental to wave
           its wand of reduction.

Aren't we always waltzing between something
and nothing?

Sparrows work the privet branches, feather
                    red and gold, don't give a shit about
        our *more-ness* or *less-ness*.

They are buoyant, sturdy, dunking
                    and soaring, disrupting
        the sky and its container of clouds.

P.B.

domino lines

Domino artist and YouTuber Lily Hevesh set a world record for domino lines using 15, 524 dominos that took two days to build and just over five minutes to collapse. It's not unlike the placing of 2.3 million blocks of limestone and granite in the Great Pyramid of Giza over a ten-to-twenty-year period. It's not unlike a series of interconnected epistles between two poets attached at ventricles and cerebella. Neither is afraid to crack open an artery in the heart, let it spill, to take a scalpel and slice the length of a dendrite to view the crystalline mass. They are willing to suffer the consequences, have the patience to watch shattered bones heal, watch gouged flesh regenerate. They are equally as willing to have their eyes widened by riding the opiate trails of extinct birds able to carry them along unknown pathways. We pretend to etch and engrave our ancient stories into the surface of large blocks, small dominos, as if they were our own stories, as if they haven't been circling our universe endlessly, an eternal recurrence, as if they were fresh and ours alone. Each cycle we learn to say goodbye, prepare ourselves for what returns, what is remade.

J.P.

the fixed and the falling

Dominos trail the living room, march the length of tiled hallway,
        strut to the counter. Charlie, my nephew who's four,
                relishes assembly and destruction.
    Slight as a sparrow,
    flings himself from chairs, countertops,
    steep dives from sofa spine, heathen blur
    on jungle gym. He terrifies me.

I've never been good at falling, bright shame
        of Merthiolate swiped on skin, scabs of indiscretion
                saved, a war of wounding at every tumble.

My body isn't a graceful thing. I'm double-jointed,
        twisting patella, discs loose as juju beads.
                Stand straight, I was told, as if being vertical, fixed
                    in place, might save the fall.
But I couldn't be contained, had to push
    against every terror.

Did I tell you I once jumped from a plane at 14,000 feet?
        Harnessed to an ex-paratrooper who earned his medal
            in 'Nam, cradled me as we somersaulted
            backwards from the hatch, falling away, falling
                like I've never fallen, falling through
            the big empty
                        then stretched out like a starfish
                        in the mist—an unbearable float.

        I was glad for the weight of him pressed
            against me. I think I might have died otherwise.

Cord pulled, we swayed like the point
        of a pendulum, wide arcs over small habitations.

The sky climbed inside me, blew me up balloon-like,
        and still, I fell.

Some of me scattered before we touched
        down and my knees buckled.
                It's adrenaline, he whispered into my ear.
                Best drug in the world.

He held me after,
        after the harness no longer strung us together.

Do you sense the sky climbing inside you? Widening the spaces,
        pumping your stories full of helium, pushing
            them out your eyes and ears.

I'll fill the air between us with words, stories
        fixed and falling. I won't learn to say goodbye.

P.B.

so many things
we haven't told each other

You haven't told me what terrifies you. But I know. I know when you walk out the door in the mornings, Hazel well-leashed, that you worry about the early morning mugger, about the leash slipping from her neck, about a large wave that sweeps you both away, about the poem oozing its way from your brain in all its imperfection. You are worried about the Covid landing on your shoulder and finding a way into your lungs. You worry about my hospice worker and whether she's up to the task of me. You wonder if we'll reach a self-imposed goal of fifty epistles shared back and forth, wonder if I will have the time, if I can pay attention well enough and long enough to mine the platinum strung together between your words. It's what you haven't told me that terrifies me, keeps me glued to the cockpit, afraid to make the final leap, a refusal to fall the 14,000 feet we both know is needed to complete the journey. No. You didn't tell me. I don't know if redwood splinters from a new deck fester under your skin. I don't know if you hid in the back of a dark closet when the lightning strikes riddled the mountains around us. Or if when the flames came, you got in a plane and headed for a distant island. I hadn't heard about the starfish, now can't get it out of my head. I know we will still hold each other after the harness no longer strings us together.

J.P.

surge

I need a new word for terror.
> For the act of being terrified. An uninhibited
>> word—one that suggests possibilities instead of fracture.
>> Like *shed*. To shed.
>> Shedding skin cells—40,000 a day, epidermal
>>> release. Something survives.

Or *surge*. I like surge even better—haunting
> movement. The tsunami surges toward me, inside
>> me, gathers me in its frigid
>> folds, tumbles bones, depletes oxygen,
>> clobbers the shit out of me.
> She didn't drown. She surged!
> Ascended the body's grief.

My surges are indigenous, soul-born mechanics. I'm a loner
> who can't be alone.
>> Empath, too full of feeling to feel.
>> Writer who mistrusts language.

To quell the surges, I must develop immunity, shrug
> inhibition. Let every terror (*yes, terror!*) loose on the page
>> to run the 500 meter in fifty seconds flat.
I'm afraid of making a mess. Chaos. Puzzles—
> their disparate pieces
> —all that's left undone, unfinished.

I'm afraid of bobcats, vultures, and the bulbous
> bodies of wild turkeys. Stinging creatures.

Osteoporosis. I'm afraid of losing Hazel, tug of leash,
fierce forgiveness. My sanity—is it too much for her to hold?

Having no one to touch, my hands sticking
to imagination alone. Already, I can't sleep
without attaching myself to Kip. Forehead
to forehead, knees jammed into groin. Sometimes, I drag
his limbs over me, want to be pinned
to the mattress. I want weight.
To be weighted. To be held in place.

What did Dorianne write?
The way death makes the air obvious in an empty chair.
I'm afraid of another empty chair.

P.B.

lure

In the early 1990s, the Coca-Cola Company invented a new soft drink, Surge, to compete with Pepsi's Mountain Dew. It was citrus-flavored and said to have a more "hardcore" edge. It disappeared from the market in 2003, apparently needing seventeen more years to further develop its attraction, to offer more caffeine per ounce than most other drinks, and explode back onto the scene with the same orange, green, and black logos. I don't drink either the Mountain Dew or the Surge. I leave the caffeine to others. I do like to watch. Like to see how they crunch cans against their foreheads. How the sugar rushes through their bloodstream to boost any tendencies toward diabetes. Wonder how sixteen ounces of liquid can make such an instant and unnatural spike in one's attitudes, one's views towards politicians and members of the opposite sex. Is it all about money and greed and who can have more of something than everyone else? When I think of Surge, I immediately occupy the costume of the Hulk and watch myself burst through tight t-shirts and pants as my muscles move beyond my control. I think of inventing my own drink. My logos would include red, and silver, and blue, have some hint of blood and metal. The marketing department is working on the name now, something like Urge, or Swell, or Lure, maybe no name at all, just a large sword that when removed explodes the powerful drink into one's throat like the shaken beer cans of our youth.

J.P.

forgiveness

I'm drawn to what is sharp. *Jian*, Chinese straight sword
      I bought years ago,
          curl of wooden hilt in my palm, love for the melodic
              language of air divided.

I was trained to fly the sword—lashing,
          striking, stabbing, snapping, stirring, splitting.
             Trained to create wide-open
    spaces where none previously existed.

In Blue Dragon Emerges from Sea, blade drawn against
          grey sky, plunge, release, slide intention
             to the tip of the sword.
          Rising round to Embrace Tiger's Head
             or the deadly parry Wind Blows Lotus Leaf,
             Lady Scatters Flowers, Bee Enters Hive.

In my dreams, attackers are man-shaped, translucent,
          pliable, made of marshmallow or pale dough. I sink
             my blade between ribs, sever arteries,
               but there is no rip or resistance, no blood,
               no blue body.

The unconscious must work out the morality of harming
          another living soul, Sifu says.

But what of sharp words—fissures
          and hammers, pointy ends of the uttered?

Feral thoughts splitting out—egoic mind dealing
its dung of defense. How small I am inside
this creature self,
animal of want and must have.

Sifu says I'm a sieve, leaking chi.
I want to touch everyone, to lure, be loved
despite offenses, agendas, failures.
I'm working on forgiveness.

Did you know that the Chinese *hanzi*
for the term martial arts
are characters for *stop* and *fighting?*

P.B.

IV.

green

What is the word for an unanswered letter?

I dug up a plant today, a species I can't recall.
    All year, its fibrous roots shunning attempts at revival.
        Greenlit for a day or maybe just an hour.
        I wasn't always paying attention.

    Brown came like erasure, consuming rust,
        punitive darkness. I took the last living
    follicles, tossed them into the bin, raked
        the hole with my fingernails, certain
weevils and their ingenious drills were to fault.

But I found no crippling
disease in the soil, no inherent enemy.

I want green—a life line. Not any line.
    I want Shakespeare's *salad days.*
        Neruda's *verde esperanza.*

    I want the green of a tiny island, seafoam,
    chartreuse, tortoise green, tenor green,
    dragon-scale green, hubris green.

Even at this distance, I see emerald, tourmaline,
    Xanadu, flushing out the cancerous
cells in your body. I don't want to replace you.

What buoy can I give you to hold on to?
What word is your life line?

Approbation. Effervescence. Domino.
Or perhaps *perichoresis*—
union of the Father, Son and Holy Ghost.

Tell me and I'll slip the word under your right hip,
        behind your scapula, in the cave-like concha
           of your ear.

I'll write it a million times in *Sanskrit,* fold it into a green
        origami throne
           so you may recline upon it.

What word will lift you? What shall I plant?
Tell me. Now.

P.B.

notes

The final line in the poem "how wind travels" is excerpted from the following verse by the Sufi mystic Rumi: "Everyone is so afraid of death, but the real Sufis just laugh: nothing tyrannizes their hearts. What strikes the oyster shell does not damage the pearl."

In the poem "surge," the line "The way death makes the air obvious in an empty chair" is taken from Dorianne Laux's poem "The Student."

The poem "green" is inspired by Natalie Diaz's epistolary poem "From the Desire Field."

acknowledgements

We gratefully acknowledge the journals who previously published the following poems: *Red Wheelbarrow:* "Between Worlds" "More than Two," "Domino Lines," "The Fixed and the Falling"; *Chicago Quarterly Review:* "How Do You Spell the Sound of Crickets?" and "This Body Yet Lives."

I want to thank Elizabeth McKenzie, Kathy Chetkovich, Paul Skenazy, and Karen Wallace for their skilled editing of this manuscript and for so thoughtfully and generously attending to every detail of this work.

Special thanks to Dorianne Laux for seeding the original idea for the project. And a heartfelt thanks to Danusha Laméris who read early drafts of my poems. I could not ask for a more wonderful or more talented mentor to gently shepherd me through the art and craft of making poems.

To my husband, Kip Allert, who understands my madness and loves me anyway. I would have no words without you.

And to my friend Jory Post, thank you for believing.

about the authors

Paola Bruni is a writer, wife, and doggie mom living on California's Central Coast. She is a two-time Pushcart Prize nominee, winner of the Morton Marcus Poetry Prize, and winner of the Muriel Craft Bailey Poetry Prize judged by Ellen Bass, as well as a finalist for the Mudfish Poetry Prize. Her poems have appeared in such journals as *The Southern Review, Ploughshares, Five Points Journal, Rattle, Massachusetts Review, Comstock Review* and *Catamaran Literary Reader,* among others.

Jory Post was an educator, writer, and artist who lived in Santa Cruz, California. He and his wife, Karen Wallace, created handmade books and art together as JoKa Press. His two books of poetry, *The Extra Year* and *Of Two Minds*, were followed by the novel *Pious Rebel* and *Smith: An Unauthorized Fictography*, a collection of fictional interviews. *Daily Fresh*, a collection of essays written during his final summer of life, was published in 2021. His work has been published in *Catamaran Literary Reader, Chicago Quarterly Review, Rumble Fish, The Sun,* and elsewhere. His short stories "Sweet Jesus" and "Hunt and Gather" were nominated for the Pushcart Prize.

you might also enjoy

Daily Fresh by Jory Post
In the summer of 2020, the final summer of his life, Jory Post gave himself an assignment: He would write one essay a day, inspired by whatever caught his eye and imagination.

Pious Rebel by Jory Post
After her partner dies suddenly, Lisa Hardrock realizes how little she knows about the life she's been living — and starts exploring her questions in a blog that unexpectedly goes viral.

Smith: An Unauthorized Fictography by Jory Post
In this kaleidoscopic, episodic joy ride, Jory Post treats us to thirty interviews that may or may not be real, with an array of "ordinary" people who turn out to be anything but, all of them in conversation with an interviewer who is herself a mystery.

CPSIA information can be obtained
at www.ICGtesting.com
Printed in the USA
JSHW021943170722
28205JS00003B/154